EVIDENCE

EVIDENCE

Art Lange

Acknowledgments:

Some of these poems have appeared, in various forms, in
Partisan Review, Sun & Moon, Washington Review, Chicago
(European Edition), *432 Review, Oink!, Mag City, The World,
ZZZZZZ*, in the anthology *15 Chicago Poets* (Yellow Press),
and in the chapbook *Glee: Song* (ad hoc press).

Publication of this book is supported by a grant from the
National Endowment for the Arts in Washington, D.C.,
a federal agency.

Library of Congress Cataloging in Publication Data

Lange, Art, 1952-
    Evidence: poems.

    I. Title.
PS3562A48486E9   811'.5'4   81-11377
ISBN   0-916328-15-5   AACR2

Design: Miles DeCoster
Photo of Art Lange: Alan Axelrod
Typeset at Word City: Chicago Print Center

Yellow Press books are distributed by
Small Press Distribution, Inc.
1784 Shattuck Avenue
Berkeley, California. Address all orders to them.

The Yellow Press
2394 Blue Island, Chicago, Il 60608

As always, for Sib
and now Christopher

Contents

E V I D E N C E

TO MYSELF

"flocculations of cirrus hang" morose
and slovenly
glistening wet amid dense grey
panels of daylight spending
black hours over an unclean
line dreaming
deep and lovely labyrinths

POEM

Not short, an oblong
presence, inviting
exaggeration
of day's design
like buildings
aligned
to avoid
the familiar. Slow
down I tell
myself. Morning
coffee dictating
the direction
of your passion, close
the canvas
curtains, looking
for a word
heard a heavy
fog with
accents, anxiously
awaiting
the cold, joy, tang
to take you
to another
place where we
walked once
while wishing
changes, along
the river, in mist,
grey, like
London and discussed
Richard III. No need
to explain the stout
and slender times
since then. Sky harder,
younger, seems
preoccupied
though able to infuse
me with its
red, its orange
buzz. Cezanne,

I never thought
I'd see
you here! A precise
personal light pointing
toward the contagious
surf, where I sleep
inspired by rocks
and stuff
in hopes like heaps.

AFTER CHINESE POETS

Snowlike yellow moon nightlight
hangs here, an almost empty mind colliding
with the hulk
of hard work, noise, paintings on the walls
a mere capricious air, empty
bottle on the low table, total anxiety
over lack of mail. The sky
ten thousand shades of blue
and bright like new
money, a pure and transparent presence
brilliant, but a ghost
of your particular mouth. Meanwhile
books pile up. Smoke
gets in my eyes.

TO YOU

Distilled and refined through the exquisite (to
exit) gracefully on the sensual resonance of
something entirely unique: obsessive,
possible and impossible effects, and the
progression sounds strangely familiar:
technique and a particular inner fire
fixed on static notes and ostinato figures
and the reason why facing you is a
dexterous skill and a passionate feeling.
Well, one suspects they all fuse together,
the different moods and fragments from
the past bobbing into view like eddies and
ripples in a river. Our playing is a precise
position which is at once steady and vulnerable.

HISTORY

Moments of obvious orange, incorrigible mists
of antiquity make one feel as if
he held a wicker head. Be seated.
A hemisphere resides in saturnine moments,
maudlin paintings allow the radiator
freedom of movement, just as
Isolde is not difficult, if one has
comfortable shoes. Episodes, therefore, revolve
around the clandestine figures and horror of
schools, oranges, and snow in its violent
sensibility. An idea, a form, a warm
February morning perplexed arrows pointing
up above heads to the point
above the point we vex as the mood strikes us.

TRUST

It takes a long
time to hear and
then you cannot put

it into words.
These things are not
limitless. The sly brim

covers the lying
eyes. Too clever, with
wide smiles actually

bacteria. Ultimately
you will be saturated
with starlight. It's

a complication.

SOLO

The first summer days shift and smack
the streets with truancies so elastic they
squirm in imitation of a collision
of stars: ecstatic sounds pound
visage bend vision crook figure deflate
parachute spill hot coffee on your lap like
a drunken linguist might if he had had
a sense of theatre or having appeared
in a film made by Rudy Burkhardt sometime
during the 1940s, lighting a cigarette
at the canvas edge of things, carelessly
tossing away the match in the manner
of thoughts grown stale in the mind, then
watching as the Big Top is consumed by flame.

SONNET FOR THE SEASON

The wistful vistas are living in objects
without fuss, a lovely talent, fur-lined with
impudent grace, evidence an old-fashioned notion
though modest, walking while longing
to levitate, to get some air, a trace
like pulling teeth out of the wind or lighting
an expatriate's cigar; though never nudge you
with their face, some information
we digest, a Callas nostalgia, oboe blunder,
orgy of casual haltingly hovering through space,
over weather, simplifying and acknowledging
the distances we keep from each other, red
and green something bulging with wonders lent:
wet, crouched, beautifully recalcitrant.

POLICE GAZETTE

Once you start something, how do you propose
to stop? First a brief jaunt
inside an episode that involved a stranger
breaking his dentures on his own pipe suddenly
made a splash in the newspapers. The former
with a looming face, a quick slipping glimpse,
"dump a tree in front of you," tidy wilderness,
bucolic women relax snugly painted
shimmering reflections dapple their forms
like a nauseous witness viewing a line-up: the faces
"not timeless icons but today's cuties." In 1960
he said very firmly "I'm no country
dumpling," while vacationing inside the People's
Republic and we discussed the war and Bertrand Russell.

YOU

I will
attempt to describe
you. Hunger

and vaguer. A deep
voice in live
rock. Green.

Entire bolts
of voluminous
pistachio.

Erect. Undulatory
coiffure. Eyelids
glowing red

through
smoke. Dirty
laundry. A pale

and gigantic
fungus. The loveliest
of beings.

LATELY

These days lacking light strangely
fascinating I have forgotten to shave
my schedule in order to remain here
standing, thinking, stepping back
plugged into a total release near the French
windows to avoid the juicy street
of the moment: filled with intimate
thoughts, a secret conversation, a vague
emotion, a breath, distracted from a possible
dream by those hung-over goons
who send dark blue telegrams which tender
the night they encompass among delicacies
completely spent, a bruise
like gauze, the drama of our lack.

SPURT

Cursory, purple, other, joyous, times as if
it's the first day of Spring, 1968, why
don't I remember? Now it's lost, gone without
song (elegant Ellingtonia *Poor Butterfly* squalid
black); the year begins hasty without soil,
a certain slant of light, cursory, purple, glimpse
of dirge a slight absent situation. Dilapidate.
Inelegantly succor, surreptitiously rapt threading
clutter out of landscape, limestone feeling
fidget. Lack of recall as if stolen, paint
part warm history of letters, fondle warm orb
of human, bolt from memory, organ music, a voice
from darkness answers: "miracles work better than
appointments" or a curiously ambivalent sense of love.

BOSTON

Back to work. To wake
where I am, almost globular,
grope, cloth over scotch skin
rasp, gulp liquid, checking cheese

for mold, flesh on chairs. Her
wet orange silk stands
in hindsight, suits
my needs. Begin to swing, pieces

of face twisting down
the drain on their way
to the ocean. Quickly sun
sings through curtain shade, from

couch scratch, motorcycles on
the rooftops. Streets trapeze takes
you by the throat, through window
blare, a music you want badly

to love. Notice how the soloist
wanders through the past, eager
to please. Don't step on the
turtle. Dictionary open, definition

of "syntax" no help, soup, orange
juice, cigarette, any clear
thing that blinds us with
surprise. Wind scraping neglected

chin, mid-day stomach full of
rocks and Mexican gas, a friend's
finger in the eye, a deficiency
of you here, home in a hot heart, tart

Cambridge has a lovely sound.

SONNET AFTER RILKE

Black bushes as a signal floating
suddenly in the ephemeral air like fame
and in the anxiety of the long year
our playing of pure
song is existence. Watching over us like rain
our muscle of infinite reception stays
tensed in the still star's blossom of possibility
within the horizontal yellow, dazzlingly
about a body of nothing but light, so soft
this hybrid of dumb strength and kisses becomes
a current bearing the head and heart
and the sweetness of ripening danger so suddenly
that sleep seems strange to us. That night
I write my memory of a day in Spring: frenzy in white.

POEM

Reading for the
first time
old poems not

mine listening
to the music
of Gabriel

Faure
for a
moment I realize

the eyes have
it
I can no

longer claim any
virtuosity other than
this that's happening

accidentally
on a February
night a considerate

and quiet voice
mentions
something about ornamentation

softly
diverse
but I find

myself too nervous
to write details I
find myself

trying in
vain
to memorize

something once
said
by Virgil

Thomson

ZERO

1

The fiesta falters from too much
upholstery. Human aspect munching
a climate too ample, a baroque grope
of head enveloped in magic. Fluent
as a grudge, sliced thumb from paper
cut, one hour of levity tenderly tweaks
the arboretum. Description of star
as a bonfire of brevity.

2

The producers of crisp worried sunlight halt
a heart, eyes a tender shutter, cleavage
of memory mirrors mute bent ambition
nailed to an ocean wave. Some secret
concern skirts sound structure like walking, like
dozing, like rusting ice. Coffee grounds frozen
into whims of anticipation, shedding
information on angles a little like lips.

3

A surprise surrounds the sky's queue, angels lack
vagueness, their rape gapes ghosts of the streets in
falsetto, recreates dinner guests on gently
reddish imitation yawn, disguised endless
city afternoon flat echo puzzle scheme, sneeze
unknowing air curling canvas into ear feast, kills
caution landscape into canon of desert and
chimes, already drenched in the perfume of love.

SECOND SONNET AFTER RILKE

Will transformation. We
liked the white
that helped feed on you. The earth
from far away the god is the place
that heals. Torn open by us ever and
again, only the dead drink...
we always overtake... all things want to float
but straight. Dance the orange
in the trampled meadow, see that you
forget what you know
about the creature that does not
exist. One horn. And this gave the
creature such strength, it took away the days.
We are only what we praise.

POEM

Some who are uncertain compel me
toward small blue serge paintings or uncontrollable
satisfaction like an enraged
winter night of lights or darkness of a moment's
grace: resplendent though slight
and fortunate enough in thrall
to be launched into dreams like a waterfall
or a subtle attraction to a life
lived in a calligraphy of casual
haste: words which come shyly
into this shadowy nuance of place
and I recognize it like a friend's face
in the way Sartre says that Giacometti "... takes
the fat off space."

LE TOMBEAU DE FRANK O'HARA

What sky! and I remember suddenly
as the head jerks (left side, eyes open), then
looking out the window one spies Glazunov heard
at the bookstore old in the rusty sounds
of summer browns of Breughel fastidious and slow
footsteps in the Five Spot Orchestra Hall cigarettes
Strega cardigans cognac the New York Times
obituary's on love. Driven to various hypnotic
dives, the precise shape of quartets and symphonies
remain our mirror, solely because we
forgive so easily. And floating through a day
of concise movement like a solo clarinet hot and
asking "What does anyone have that we
don't?" eating March 21st lentil soup

IOWA CITY SERENADE

for A.A.

Cello depths dye
the streets I borrow
from devoutly to
survive

this drought, a debt
of mind forever
unpaid, unraveling
amid Victorian

splendors transported
at no uncertain
emotional expense
from deep

in Davenport, miles
into Moline's misty
mycosis: 3 AM cobwebbed
lamplight dusty International

Harvester habitual morning
wheeze by ghost-
like perpetual
sneeze over greasy

hash-browns bourbon
bled subsequently sotto
voce at the
Deadwood. The old

one, that is. And
could I please
return to those
thrilling days

of yesteryear, *por
favor?* ...to cut
the fuse
and agonize over

the alchemy
which defines
us, Ducal
fashion, til the Hawk

reminds us, it'll
be blue
skies, like blue
cellophane,

from now on?

THREE AFTER KEYS

1

Waking at noon with every step a cold
dawn breaking, habitual cough, blur followed
by Cezanne streaking through the quiet
streets of Aix shouting *"Le Monde, c'est
terrible."* What we were a year ago I do
not know, though shimmering and
somnolent. It's not unusual to wonder why
we never want to reread Proust, bathed in blue
fluorescent light cerulean where the night
ends, gremlin eyes mixed with mine
outside the blinds. The streetlamp
flaps with a worn-out mystery sizzling half-
heartedly, I see Cezanne's sins under a tree
sit severed and soiled, somewhere in Chelsea.

2

Difficult to recall local
air, clouds meatier
than trees
at Newport where I go
in homage to the old
eschatology. Red with
rain, I tire of mind
residue, assume
the frigid position while
dreams I know
I've had burn and glow,
hang in the sulphured
snow snug, old scars
that merge like a piano
played four hands; notes
not composed, but those
I penciled on the
landscape, frantic with
failure but proud
of the penmanship.

3

Green some afternoons, others brown
prematurely without reason. Authorities warn
against vertical and warm seasons April'd
with enjoyment, instead always August empties
elusive in the face of wet silk light a severed
head of blue hue true to an opened vein, ambition
dissolving to a sluggish shadowed bulge
absorbed by the continual entourage of sandwich
boards interrupted only by rare vain gumption.
"Warum?" asks Franz Schubert, habitually inhuman
fingertips run over rue, ruthlessly arpeggiating
through outline of signs' clang neon lightning-like
over Viennese law offices: *Chess Problems Solved.*
Though it's a game you can't not be involved.

"Now that things are so simple there's so much
to do." And to bed, for no purpose
other than recognition through creativity. The bed
situated in one pale corner of narrow quarters
where on occasion anyone might show up. Even
the enemy. Drinking seemed a natural consequence
considering the conversation which struck the heart
like a sardonic bullet. Next day to bed.

Next day a curious hopeless calm. Next day January.
Next day philosophy. Nancy described a zeppelin raid:
a young woman in white silk on a small stage:
it was tiresome. Next day captured by the enemy.
Our pale moon awry. Next day thighs.

"He possessed an incredibly acute and subtle ear."
All I could do was listen, poor mood, linear, grey.
He revealed all too brilliantly how the hand was offered
and food put to the mouth. He was blue
in the face. Fortunately the ear clears what the eye
fears.

BLACK SALAD

Lifted from a swan's wing once occasionally sung
overheard but upon entering upright with rare aplomb
the amateur *hauteur* of morning smack with elusive
fist to nose. Nobody home, walk the streets,
gorge on pure air, while frigid internal rain
freezes and sleets to a golden gloom, in another
room eyeing store window dummies new clothes for
entertainment? Rolling cigarettes galore under
moonlight veneer of urgencies false and
otherwise, thoughts purely anxious and whiney,
translations of sun tease the "poet as tourist."
Plenty of broom for fragrance and color raised in
dream-cleaning, fumbling among the double
lives lived bloodless, evanescent as a bubble.

FAVORS

It's time, again. I'm waiting for Peter, and
the mail, though I know "you're not supposed
to expose those things:" the jingle of darkness
in a conventional city. I'm embarrassed with
Summer (pleasure a debt unpaid) incredibly cluttered.
In the conjuring comes clouds clasped on a label,
occasionally hidden, authentically fresh, laconically
apt. On the other hand, I cling to a ragged flight
along empty space, engaging in social intercourse
with photographs of stars, their indifference anything
but dandy. Notes no help, in between the times spent
stoking the fires which the season savors, the same
piece of favorite film explodes on the couch, dream
orchestra chomping at the end of my touch.

SONNET

Tod und das Mädchen Op. Posth. Ein
Deutsches Requiem Op. 45 Meerestille und
glückliche Fahrt Op. 112 Les Francs-Juges
Op. 3 Francesca da Rimini Op. 32 La
Stravaganza Op. 4 Ouvertüre zu A.V. Kotzebues
Festspiel "Konig Stephen" oder "Ungarns
erster Wohltäter" Op. 117 Herzog Blaubarts
Burg Op. 11 Verklärte Nacht Op. 4 Begleitungsmusik
Op. 34 Saga-Drøm Op. 39 Nusch-Nuschi Tänze
Op. 20 Hin und Zuruck Op. 45a
Davidsbündlertänze Op. 6 Der Hirt auf
dem Felsen D. 965 Schwanengesang D. 957 Cosi
Fan Tutti K. 588 Thamos, König in Ägypten K.
345 Gottes Zeit ist der Aller beste Zeit BWV 106

DIVERTIMENTO

I suddenly recall two months previous sucking
squawks out of an undernourished air
with purely anxious and whiney thoughts smuggled
into a curious lucidity "we were invited"

we drink in conversation magnificently adroit
"cocktails" out the window immaculate prisms
float in a leeward tide carved out in the interior
of my eye "You can't get there from here" but dry

yourself by the fire and shake the weather
from your coat separate the sincerity from
the snow and save the former instinct spellbound
self aggressive direct and conversational while a wobbly

sun seems wicker in slow dusk, sliced, it changes
suddenly from wet to snow incorporates
cream and pearl whites as light and tender
as breath a certain simple rendering "we

were invited" ears besieged by fuzz and fire
but persists, drawn simply, with azure sparks
down dazedly speaking flatly as easily
as laying linoleum borders at the absolute

boundaries of sentences small truculent and sentimental
with an expression of surprise (sometime
during the week, living by the heart, and pugnacious
domesticity) at who appears at the party, uninvited,

a giddy imitation of nothing ever seen before
a precise personal light, particular insights,
unbelievably stubborn with rays of careless
conversation a subtle crinkle intrudes inconsequence

we go out to seek the quiet procedures but remain
"wrong from the start" charmless though dignified
anxious with thoughts of possibilities astounds
inside it is warm and snowy like a promise made

by mistake and never kept a faithful
anonymous performance a painfully faithful
performance anonymously remarkable bare in the crafty
breath of you hearing the doorbell ring or rather chime

meaning more behind the door to join in the
confrontation like meeting yourself in delicious advantage
on the street unexpectedly amid fields of flutter
noticing the room filled with people in your face

and suddenly there's Poulenc at the party, precursing
the fingerings of a peculiar nocturne difficult sublime
supplicating a contemplative incantation and listening
interestedly to an animated Tony Towle, then sadly wagging

his head in a spontaneous gesture mirroring the video
fecund magical toxic like bums travelling incognito, no end
to the purple days we hear groups of silence in the
corners, whims, more chimes, a formal spasm

while pedagogic appears lethal the seduction of things
boulevard period life monotone almost a rich panoply
intricacies and expensive cheese in the kitchen
motionless encased in a mist hazy like a spray

of ideas formed in the mouth and spit out
like sour wine into the face of the conversant, a gift
considering estuarial ardors and orbs like tendencies
abandoned, ovoid shapes held in tension rigid like

dialogue, in spurts, between two cozy bent somewhat
lame looking dulcet lately disinterested a red soft
pillow to placate interior weather dangerously vibrato
figures blur take on functional punctuation in the memory

a rude shatter of palette as everything suddenly disintegrates
dissolves disappears leaving only thin air and solid
objects forcing us to rely solely on
the wisdom of the heart, and something else.

INVISIBLE CITY SERIES

for F.D.

1

On one knee, Fielding, between
my profile, on one knee, the street
breathes that whole gang, umber streets
ragged and browner, but bright green beret
blowing, seemingly legs that go dancer.
The danger is forget style, drop
taught jab cantillations, ribs trickle,
but everyone looked a little foolish.
Behooved bleeding ribs, taking book, bite
that sheen outside white within face
windows, this gigantic spiff to be
dust and lights. The shoes fit, and with
lights opposing I clinch, married,
darkening the human eye at the center.

2

Behind the fingerprints, pauses, shakes it,
nothing urgent, a silk chandelier floats
the light, the Ink Spots above, sweat rising
behind the curtain, the hand waving, outlining
the caper. The dark behind the night in
bunches paces the edges of stockings, hanging.
The point was slowly fist, morning dense
diamonds up and running forced glass forehead
of lacerated belly. Behind slaps, legs
follow breaking the cement with her teeth.
In front of him, water on the belly.
From there, squeezes. The ear, you can
open it, the keys between the fingers, the blade
sleeps in the body, under the fingerprints.

3

In the eyes an enormous mouth drawn
to clutch at this photograph, to fade
like a flag; dim, withdrawn but wearing
rage and glinting glass blind, clearing
out space for trumpet rip like accelerating
knees tumble to meet panic by the throat...
there's nothing in his head to prevent
brilliance; searing stare...his temples
don't deserve his eyebrows, frustratedly float
unused and drink torso but head still glares
tentative under the transparent shrug and shed
night power star gravity. The moisture and
motion meet in thought float a candelabrum
slender hands vanish leisurely entangle.

4

Breathing the incision of page's nocturnal fire
fingers turn towards them to slow down
the lip of obscure framed frozen face, an object
living furnished with keys you cut and odor
from a notebook without words and tired to
voyage you let it accumulate melt with a few
careful innocuous first risky functions
alternatives is incoherent the insertions cough
without promises horns are full of victims the text
raped the calendar with a verb. The anger beneath
the skin bubbles eyes agitation casual inside
the cities bruised a pool table with some
enthusiasm vegetates clarity excites the
instruments open the head consider the cordial.

5

Tuesday the pressure was on. Plato
called but couldn't find one cheaper than
an Argentinian fairy. He treated her
like a lady she said. On Thursday
the pressure raided the hovel to see if Harlow's
footprints were still there. She wanted my
weakness, my mind, a trap teeming rain. Descartes
called to reduce the pressure. The radio
rats retreated to Berkeley in fury. The streets
coughed skyline aglow with Marx. Too hot to eat so
Bette Davis did not affirm the pressure when
Wittgenstein called her. In a week the Sahara
finished the pepsi, the sun--voiceless and human--
hearing the dark dreams of Mercury and a metallic sleep.

6

It starts thick with rust after midnight
red situation budge with daylight. Confirms
loses ethics on awakening, enjoy an agreement
of absence in which as a rule you slice
the pages extinguish psalms break fragments blown
by a breath--evidence: released voices. The horizon
steps anticipate snaps adopt stilts a honed dress
distraction on top of the lens presence burns.
Chapter persists; the rain burns color broken
conducted inertia, slender, jade peeled emerald.
Yesterday painted small cherries at the edge of
the mouth of Po Chu, like lips in a back pocket
drawn by the times. Sketched in black-and-white on
page one your liquid accordion. I feel green whim.

7

All night up and walking through decorative
whites and blacks, several sources of incessant
purely personal plus two eyes fills a life
work capable and decorative measured from will
to despair--I can't pay my rent but there's
trouble at the tonal edge. After long
hesitation I lie absolutely certain and smoked.
First stop a just benevolence; drear warm kitchen
caught sight diagonally of small bar and brass
choir. Stingy with oysters, disfigured by guzzle, swam
the square cutting a seventeenth-century figure:
portraitist in front of a colonnade, this window. Later,
tasting the generic, fearing scurry, silk luminous
that becomes electric stride in city physical.

(from) COMPOSITION

Day grows rapidly suspended in time
in vacant space its long advancing column
lofty like luminous day, when the world was weak.
Like the clashed edges of two words we wore

on our fingertips, without magnificence.
In the cold weight of winter you are yourself
I am someone else. And am affirmed
someone else in vague terms burning like brandy

amid the intimacies of strangers in a silent street
that living in air symbolized the departing adventure.
But the inner compulsion dropped out of this
dream, voiceless and soft, leaving only what you see,

mostly memory. Its veiled withdrawal
rises from land and sea to obliterate depths,
the composition of blue sea with heavy ease.
The inhuman making choice that fosters resolve--

lakes are more reasonable, unconscious of love
or look, standing you look on stars.
Not your silent selves soft in your dreams
but imageless and projecting the long channels

to recreate the watery words. A waveless sea
a ship that reels when the womb widened
so that we feel and feeling it around you
becomes the sea it falsifies

and will starve at last on the blue waste.
And you, reckless in the dim rooms
are not now near, in the flush and height
in a confusion of fire, awaiting its end.

Secreted until then and wound in the imminence
we shall forget by day to see,
this is its essence: a ripening gladness
jotted down in the dark under empty covers

like a carving in space withholding light
while lighting the obscure word; lounging life wholly
like a whore, enduring a rancorous heart
and substituting stratagems of the spirit for

a surface pain. In the quiet there
they talk of the weather; it happens.
Day, night and man shaking off doubt
laid in the leaves bitten by blizzards

suspended in air behind the quiet house.
It is as if there were a hired bed
and bright, a jar phosphorously kept
in a dim low-raftered room suspended in air

as nothing ever is. But if there be something
suspended in air it be perfect fear
escaping each morning but gaining its strength
in a senseless syllable seeking the nerve

of nearer water--a visible hole
or cancerous morning space in the embrace.
And small, in the spasm of the mood
in a world of ideas stillborn on the table

of imagination. Now in my ear
a souvenir in solid fire flickering
under high fractured cliffs. As the eye closes
the clamorous ear pursues the curve of the body

so avid and nude and beautiful and so you
like the sky over the graveyard.

AFTER CRAVAN

More than scuffle, its color and place
trace around the rim of that space, at the edge
of your hesitation. Tomorrow is that face,
severe and withdrawn, though you are still
eligible. The better part of day accepts you
as numerous as the shifting curve of
the window curtain, slanting its certain
stream invisible on its departure to stretch
a nose, pale and realistic as holds an
afternoon of lace hollow and sinuous. You forget
the nameless things that bind you to this race:
your career, your images, its passion a trace
scattered as you inhale a case of hard night,
the hour your boredom first saw the light.

AUGUST, EARLY

In red neglect rent
now from the order of the universal whose
back is bent
to the bubbling fountain--choose
an easy power, stay out of sight,
a number of partnerships refused? Commands
bend the back, the weather's changing, bright
browning of clusters, hands you a
towel of rhododendrons (you said they
plot in alliance) and make you shudder
on my arm. "It's a man's
duty!" the radio said--and you, without
a head. "On your feet!" The oboe
solo. Today I suddenly believe.

TANGO

                         birds
          smoke   is that so? someone says
"height begins from the ground" more smoke
                begin festivities   spurt
     of clutter residence implies cling
                implies absence . . . explode
of components seriously comma pewter magnificently
          adroit   how
                 often do you occur? condition of throat
          imported cigarettes gift
wrapped in the arms of a saxophone introducing
                              a pummel of air
          frescoes procedure we hit
          on accidentals we say
                      something to someone we
don't recognize samurai to love a word
                miraculously succinct miraculously
          adept miraculously contrary tenuous liquid
                      part orange passion part myth
          a few murky notes stand in flying mirror
smile smoke marimba later laughingly
                khaki   superb when laughter
          of strangers on a journey
                with "ghost of a chance" annoyed snapshot

"do you play
Othello?" beloved though behind the eight
ball "do you play pool?"
relax exaggerations exclaim stop
abruptly dominate space hesitate voice
sense of guest and growing overlap the
elastic but tickets were impossible to come
by   so room echo sum shifts trombonish
search concrete confront power
assertion weight shifts dramatic to free
danger viable trio alternating clipped ellipsis
of articulation hard to vital
so near   so needs
reed section short to call the crust what
was meant to do
shouting find "found" has ceased
burlesque measured again repetition negligee creased
to be event in sorcery soothe
noun something on much smoke widespread
other from birds touch years to doubts. seriously
bells

SUDDENLY

Everything in this place where language lives
seems as redundant as the dream orchestra
nudged by thuds as dull notation sheds
viciously upon conventional instruments
of imitation: no illusion without radiance
torn through the tedium of sincere collages
within this ambitious distribution of
seemingly random placement of forms
so much depends upon
the suction within collections
rising and striding out of the remembrance
of lovely mathematics at whose behest
at the end of this geometrical day one
suddenly notices fresh desecrations of the portico.

CHAGRIN

There's a poem by Yeats, I'm not sure
quite which one it is, something
guarding the mirror, and *On Bear's Head*
you might imagine, while reading Yeats
about old mummy wheat, horrible green
allegro combined with an heroic couplet,
birds, and a sound sleep. No, it's the
sound of stamping hooves, more truly
andantino movement of the Debussy string
quartet. Being driven, abstract, to the obscure
overeducated, operatic, a sunflower. Check the ear,
check the coat, intoxicated through self-justification
pleasures which the mad Yak receives, taken
for granted to be ice water, metaphysical.

DUO

Clutter. And with a cigar down halls of Chaucer
resort to a firmness of purpose and a strength
of mind, unstable, with a sense of mild
extraordinary air conjured like quicksand. "Even
you were happy last Wednesday." In green time
titles flowered, text an ice-cold shower to an
unsuspecting me. Later toweling off, voluminous
echoes of clouds with little else to feed
on. "You know, you can't read in a dream, too
cold." Still searching for your voice, to live
within, and needing a keyboard to play it on, all
fuse the drowsy and a faint face too sparse for
space, but spark these remnants of free-fall until two
of us find ourselves in that dream which we woo.

FOR INSTANCE

Nerves thrive
on the cutting
edge

of sound, hanging
around an empty
apartment,

queasy, clear
mind of redundant
weather (a

formality) voices
of ink
function

shakily, once
in a while
spurt, a curt

reference, mull
it over, get
a haircut, keep

the faith, read
the sky a solid
grey

filled
with invisible
anger, dissolving

rainbows like
punctuation "all
right, you

two, break
it up!" listening
the slight

light slides
slants
in, dusty, paint

drying in
tubes along the
highway, a

caress
of furniture, feeling
lost in the

folds, sounds
mum, not
noticing, for

instance, that
goon noodling
on

the horn
in
the corner

N.O.Y.B.

For a while I thought I had gotten used
to it, the lyrical strands left in its
stead. We went the other way, eager
on the striped contour surrounded
by an artificial impromptu, lifting
a slogan, usually verging on electric
painting. Your body has changed into a
fictive area, like the shiny bell
of a brand new tenor saxophone. The effulgence
of your sway betrays my thoughts into a rumour
of spellbound frescoes. Nietzsche said: "The mind
is more like a stomach than anything
else." A famous movie mogul once said: "If you
have a message, send a telegram."

OPENING

Fleshed in a loop from the wrist's pulse
to the heart as urgent bells occupy morning air shyly
I hold together pieces of waiting and bolts
of memory in a fabric with the fascination
of perspective the way one views the inhuman texture
of a dead man's organ music. Thinking of a line
found in another's book, sliced,
it changes so suddenly you watch it tipple.
A simple certain rendering of colors hoist
purely casual quick references to a landscape
of sensibility under scrutiny into a moist
fleet evening theme turning into Haydn.
Fleshed in a loop from the wrist's pulse
a wobbly sun seems wicker in slow dusk.

NITWIT SERENADE

Winding down day's rhythm curiously lax
lacks crack and sizzle tonight almost caricature
in its slush for dream riff; insistent ac-
cidents of light occur in opening the refrigerator:
an egg boiled white, orange juice, cold night, later
lost in the tangle of flounces, awake, twitch knee
knowing the name which haunts mirrored in ear
merge with verve narrative filled lacy; brews BG's
discursive squealing "Bugle Call Rag" electronically
prompt mutters muster tacit towards what ends
the discussion: a line intrudes, looks dulcet, looks lately
disinterested, though bent back from Donne, lends
itself rigid, quick, hangs tough in my ear:
"These are my best days, when I shake in fear."

RUMOR

1

Sun dim with wind
chilling teeth, cloud
wears its white
suit, waiting
to burn, pale you
put on the
world, your weight
shining, and shooting
body metal features
feel strength, breathing
with the meaning
of naked, curving
pure energy, dress,
breath
deeply, wake and
walk.

2

I listened for the son
of a bitch rap, drawn
to dawn's stressing
glitter, two
eyes justify moaned
knife light bright
breaks in two, shout
shed onto pavement
cross the firm
street, ceremoniously
flame among traffic
blast
crazy as a soul,
roaring, inciting
the new
arrangement, while
wistfully plying
we imagine
dancing, dining

PLACID

>for P.K.

Air shine neatly within the boundaries of glee
felt viewing a lake or answering the telephone: a
love affair with the line, a pencil sketch of one's
attributes. Chords spurt altocumulus, so home again
slashing a batch of the screed found here; book
bent to the convenient, boiling tea, musn't do
that! But nothing can be done so slowly as to wake
within a swirl, a jar, a sort of incident. Chords
racing toward thought, extreme craggy viable ones
function gorgeously, without commotion. Spirits
harden, then hazy dissonance circumvents channels
of mood to drift in, as if to loiter in a hum,
evanescent as a bubble float lightly chords arch in air
explodes like a rose: bright moon dance in underwear.

COPENHAGEN

It is a privilege to see so much confusion.
An opaque illusion
"The visitor dare never fully speak at home
for fear of being stoned
as an imposter." Clearly defined pseudopodia.
Ghosts
          "telling me my own dream"
arrive here in such thick

"Disobedient persons being summarily removed
and not allowed to return without permission in writing."

must avoids:
a closing of eyes
seldom successes
and complaisancies
described by the cartographer of 1539.

We should like to know how that was done.

The work of careful men with shovels.

FRAGMENT

Grey city day so
nearly genuine finds
concussion in the
orange graced blank

space hot coffee
fills; the gift
of gab gone with
autumn bright

under December's
drift, fret. I quit
shaving several
months ago, though

you never
know
about these
things. Color clings

to doubt
at desk,
edgy, twitching, thoughts
in total

disarray
though those days
haze stays magnetic;
meanwhile the brown

leaves are on
the asphalt
now, a renewed
arabesque and trim

shadows swim suave
as a loon, stringent
as strychnine and
cool, complex

as air and
uglier. As
the party breaks
up, moon

delights dim
wobble white
wistful gawky
ghosts unsteady on

ice equally
enviable. Up the
avenue I sit, sandwich,
serious, books

from which I
crib, smoke,
dull roar
from keys compressed

into machinelike
wheeze, old
air expelled, a
view of winter

trees weaving
among thought
balloons with equivocal
ease. Gaudy

joys move leanly
lately along crevices
designed
devices for ricochet

calypso of sun's
interrogation--
instantly
transplanted to

Pisan's cerulean
sky blue and E.P.
surmising "It
took me 70

years
to realize I
wasn't a
lunatic, but a

moron." Slowly
things empty, stomach,
studio, street
of veins, dreams, fat

volumes of
fog, fire from
my face
drains, rains

drizzle famished, leak
leery into bleak
boulevard glistening
damp--alternatives, like

hound's teeth,
bared--flesh out
to fill a head, instead
baptized with old

brew, gorge
on glass snacks, chat
til morning stomp
attacks the cracks, but

bed neatly
negotiated, under honk-
sized moon lacquer sunk,
later sun's "random

jelly" opaque grace
soothes the day's
pace, quiets
the heart's

rattle, snakes
through lace
curtains questioning,
sharp as shrapnel,

green fallen deeply
into grass, escapes
whitely into
dream of

color flash-
lit from scratched
nerves, drowsy
monument sights slow

curves, taste like
needles frying,
here where life
is boring.

LIQUID CHESS

Walking, things go slow, wetly yet curiously
synchronous with the universe of blurs, stroking
incidental surface flash fur-like sights
freshly: rush of clusters beckon to me
as a dare, where they "dump a tree in front
of you" like a nauseous witness viewing
a line-up, the jingle of darkness in a conventional
city as you slip into the grey, stoking the fires
the season savors. Underneath some loping
new haunting suspension the sound of awkward
blue rising stridently over Second Avenue.
Intensely crowded thoughts splash fluid form
on random focus, softly scattered spilled or rather
friendly shatter, like an anthem, soar.

TO MY WIFE

A loaf of bread, believe it or not, here
next to the typewriter, the writer, tongue
burnt, mouth dry and roof raspy from beginning
pipe again, these are a few of my favorite
things--I read that somewhere once. Or a sensible
waltz by Szymanowski taught to tango til push comes
to shove, and I learn more craft, less art contagiously
like a letter lost from a lover lost. The body
fills with annoyance, fills with fastidiousness, with
coffee you offer. A tangle of tenderness
but later I loaf, an oaf of gruff and bluster
adrift on a riff Kansas City made edible. When doubts
come I waffle; this one audible, though I can't taint
my thanks to you for letting me be brilliant.

YELLOW PRESS BOOKS:

Red Wagon–Poems by Ted Berrigan
   paperback $3.00 cloth $7.95 signed $15.00

New and Selected Poems–Paul Carroll
   paperback $3.50 cloth $7.95 signed $15.00

Utopia TV Store–Poems by Maxine Chernoff
   paperback $3.00

Physical Culture–Poems by Richard Friedman
   paperback $3.00

15 Chicago Poets–Edited by Richard Friedman,
   Peter Kostakis and Darlene Pearlstein
   paperback $2.50

Letter to Einstein Beginning Dear Albert–Poems by Paul Hoover
   paperback $3.00

Carapace–Poems by Henry Kanabus
   paperback $2.50

The Hat Issue–Milk Quarterly 11 & 12, Edited by Peter Kostakis
   paperback $3.00

Evidence–Poems by Art Lange
   paperback $3.50

Alice Ordered Me to Be Made–Poems 1975 by Alice Notley
   paperback $2.50 cloth $6.95 signed $12.00

The Grand Et Cet'ra–Poems by Barry Schechter
   paperback $2.50

Catalogue available from Yellow Press
2394 Blue Island
Chicago, Illinois 60608

Yellow Press books are distributed by
Small Press Distribution, Inc.
1784 Shattuck Avenue
Berkeley, CA. 94709